With
Love,
Jonathan Ponetta
xo

be yourself

The lights come up on a bare stage.
A single dancer stands still at the center,

waiting.

As the bassoonist plays the first plaintive notes of Igor Stravinsky's *Rite of Spring*,
the dancer's torso
begins to undulate.

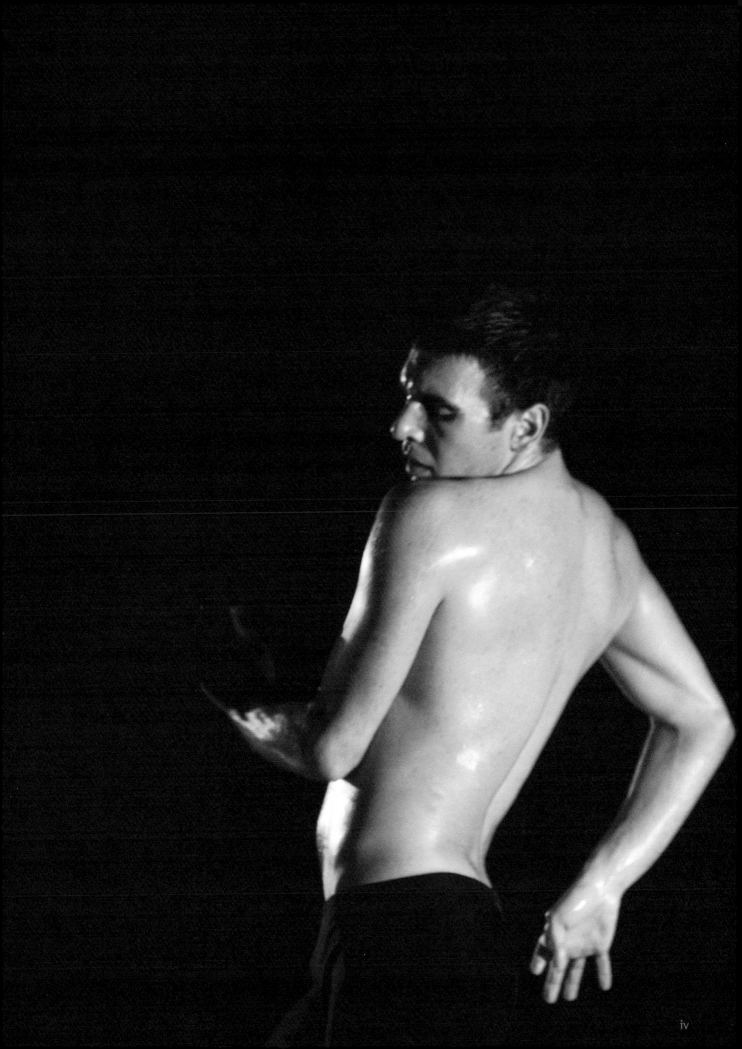

iv

Head bent slightly forward,
he extends an arm to either side.
Palms down,
he slowly lifts his shoulders,
his arms following naturally, like the wafting wings of a bird.

For more than
30 minutes,
the entirety of
Stravinsky's
ferocious score,
the dancer
leaps and spins,
his arms now
churning
like windmills,
or pumping
the air
like a boxer,
fists clenched.

The solo, choreographer Molissa Fenley's *State of Darkness*,
requires the dancer's fullest concentration.

He must master both the steps
and his own mind.

Jonathan Porretta holds the audience captive in his open hands.

When Stravinsky's final notes fade away,
Porretta comes to a full stop,
bare chest heaving, sweat dripping down his torso.

The audience leaps to its feet with an appreciative roar.

"It's an amazing piece," remarks Pacific Northwest Ballet Artistic Director Peter Boal, one of the few who has performed this marathon himself.

"What's fascinating about that solo: you see the dancer click in, you do see them lose awareness. They're doing something in space, and you're privy to watch it. But they're not doing it for you."

That inward focus is a rare occurrence in
Jonathan Porretta's career.

He lives to entertain his audiences.

He loves them more than they love him, he says.

Given the way we clap for him
after this—and every—performance,
that's hard to believe.

by Marcie Sillman; photography by Angela Sterling

Out There

Jonathan Porretta's Life in Dance

by Marcie Sillman
photography by Angela Sterling

Front-Cover Image: Jonathan Porretta in George Balanchine's *Square Dance* at PNB (by Angela Sterling)

Back-Cover Image: Porretta and his mother, Jane D'Annunzio (photographer unknown)

"Becoming Jonathan" essay © 2016 Marcie Sillman

"Becoming Jonathan" essay and *State of Darkness* "Overture" previously excerpted at KUOW.org

State of Darkness "Overture": text © 2016 Marcie Sillman; images © Angela Sterling

Roméo et Juliette "Curtain Call": text © 2016 Marcie Sillman; images © Angela Sterling

"The Highlights" text © 2016 Jonathan Porretta

Angela Sterling images © Angela Sterling (angelasterlingphoto.com)

Lindsay Thomas images © Lindsay Thomas (lindsaythomasphotography.com)

Rex Tranter images © Rex Tranter (rxtranter.smugmug.com)

Marc von Borstel images © Marc von Borstel (marcvonborstel.com)

Effort has been made to identify the original photographers except in the case of casual snapshots. Errata and additional photo credits may be found at jonathanporretta.com.

Designed and edited by Rosie Gaynor

Published by Seattle Scriptorium LLC through IngramSpark

Contents

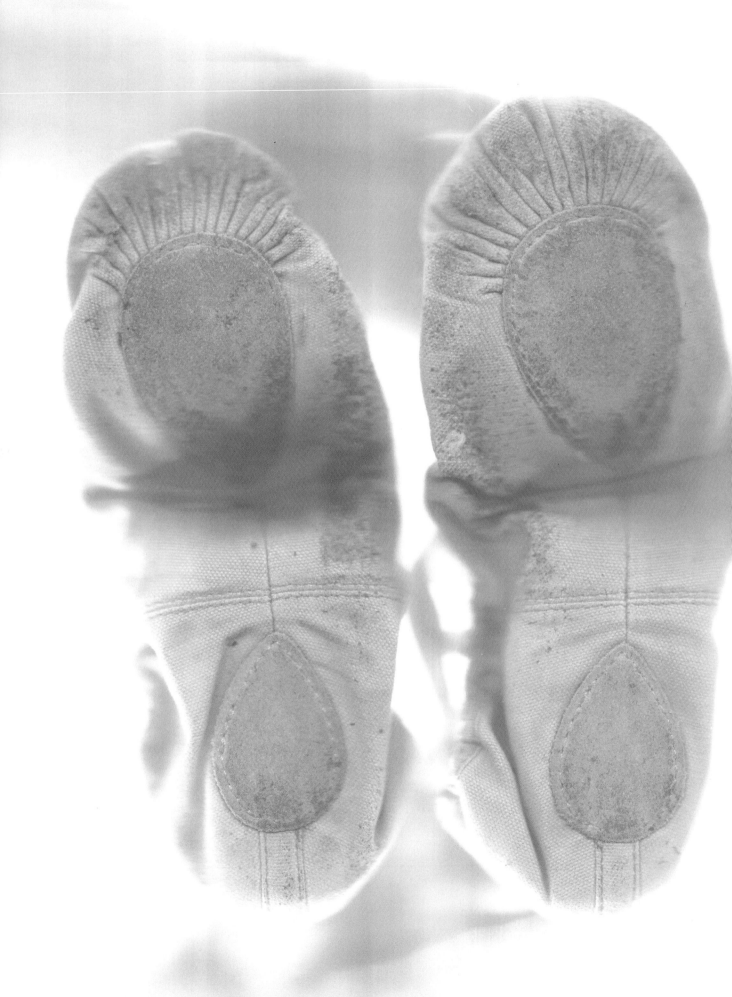

Jonathan Porretta's shoes, January 2016 (Rosie Gaynor image)

Foreword

He is so very generous. It's not just his talent, his technique, his musicality, his exuberance, and his ability to entertain that makes so many of us fall in love with Jonathan Porretta. It's his willingness to share the dance with us. When he does those turns across the front of the stage in *Rubies*—at first throwing them off lazily like any old move, and then gradually speeding up, in the end cramming in three times as many perfect turns as the remaining space allows—we feel the joke and the joy of it. And we get to feel what it's like to do something you love.

When you walk away from a Jonathan Porretta performance, you take a little of the dance with you. It's like humming a good tune after a show…except that it's your body "humming" a dance. Great party. Awesome swag!

I've left out so much: That he's sweet. And sassy. And kind. An angel; an imp. And funny and flippant and fun. And cosmically serious and sympathetic. And smart. And brave. And human.

Marcie and I, ballet buddies since we met on an NEA fellowship at the American Dance Festival seven years ago, have never tired of talking about Jonathan. The articles we've gotten to write about him just weren't enough. We wanted something longer and less ephemeral. A book! And so we met with Jonathan, to see if he'd be open to the idea.

We found out that Jonathan had something he had been wanting to say for a long time. A message to kids especially, but also to adults, about life: how it can hurt to be different, but how being yourself is really key. Be yourself, do your thing, and eventually you'll run into people who love you for who you are.

That seemed like a great idea for a book. Marcie and I ditched our fan book idea, and she signed on to write Jonathan's story. So, here it is. Don't be surprised if you find yourself "humming" a little after you read what she wrote…

—Rosie Gaynor

Becoming Jonathan

Porretta at age 9 at Totowa Dance Center
(image courtesy of Jane D'Annunzio)

Jonathan Porretta has wanted to entertain for as long as he can remember.

When he was three years old, his mother, Jane D'Annunzio, took him and his two older siblings to a New York City Ballet performance of *The Nutcracker*.

By the end of the ballet, Jonathan had fallen asleep with his head on his mother's shoulder and a smile on his face. From that day on, he told everyone within earshot he wanted to be a dancer.

It was a puzzlement to his close-knit Italian-American family.

Dance was most definitely not part of Jane D'Annunzio's world. Although she grew up just 20 miles from Manhattan, in Totowa, New Jersey, it might as well have been another planet. D'Annunzio's father was a construction worker; she ran a landscaping company.

"I drove a truck!" she says.

Porretta at ages 1, 3, 7, and 12
(images courtesy of Jane D'Annunzio)

D'Annunzio knew early on that her youngest son was different from his siblings, and from most of the other kids in Totowa. He was animated and precocious, always clowning around for his family. He'd pull on an old pair of pajamas and dance around their small, Cape Cod-style house on his chubby toddler legs.

One day, before Jonathan was even two years old, D'Annunzio had a revelation. "I remember saying to my friend one day, 'Oh my god, I think this kid is gay!'"

D'Annunzio can't explain why she thought that. At the time, more than 30 years ago, she didn't know any openly gay people in Totowa. All she knew was that her little boy was sweet and gentle, nothing like his rough and tumble older brother. And she knew that she loved him to bits.

  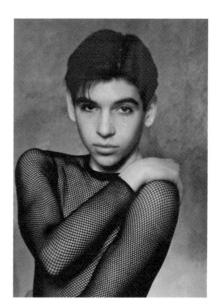

Porretta at Totowa Dance Center at age 7
(images courtesy of Jane D'Annunzio)

Jonathan continued to pester his mother about dancing. Money was tight, but for Jonathan's seventh birthday, D'Annunzio and a friend gave the boy a year of dance lessons at the Totowa Dance Center, in a nearby strip mall.

Porretta was the only boy in his class; his teacher, Miss Barbara Bruno, treated him like one of the girls. They wore sequins, he wore sequins. They dressed up as ponies or flowers and so did he. He was in his element.

"I didn't like school, growing up," says Porretta. "I couldn't talk to the kids."

But dance class was different. He and the girls shared a passion.

It was the place that felt like home to him.

Things were not so good at school. The other boys picked on him, called him names. Nobody beat him up, but nobody wanted to be his friend. Even the girls who liked him at Miss Barbara's studio snubbed him at school.

One day after school, Jonathan came into the kitchen. He asked his mother what a fag was. D'Annunzio remembers that day clearly. Her son's question stunned her, but only momentarily.

"Who said that to you?" D'Annunzio demanded. But Jonathan wouldn't answer. He didn't want to get the other kids in trouble.

D'Annunzio says, "I told him, 'Don't listen to what those kids say. Don't listen! One day you're going to be famous!'"

She can't explain why she believed that Jonathan would achieve his dream. It was just one of those things she felt to be true.

Porretta took his mother's words to heart. But every day he ate his lunch alone at what the other kids called The Losers' Table. He made friends with a lunch lady; he helped the school nurse. And he bided his time until 5:30, when he would be back in the dance studio.

———————

The word—fag—didn't mean much to Porretta when he was at Washington Park Grammar School. He didn't have boyfriends or girlfriends, or really any friends, so romance was an abstract idea to him.

But he does remember the first time he felt real love for somebody outside his immediate family. D'Annunzio had taken him along on an errand, to the garden supply center. The little boy fell asleep in his mother's truck, and she had to carry him inside when she went to make her purchases.

"One of the men who worked there said, 'Let me hold him,'" she recalls.

Porretta thinks he was seven years old at the time. "I remember waking up in this man's arms, looking up at his face and being in love with him." It seemed perfectly natural.

Unlike so many of his friends, Porretta has no coming-out story. He says he's always been gay. That's the way it is.

Porretta at age 7
(Jane D'Annunzio photo)

Like his mom, Jonathan Porretta never doubted his future as a dancer. From the age of seven, when he stepped into Miss Barbara's ballet/tap combo class at the Totowa Dance Center, he never looked back. The twice-weekly classes morphed into a daily regime of jazz, ballet, lyrical, and tap. He wanted to learn it all.

Eventually Porretta left Miss Barbara's school. He'd fallen off his bicycle, breaking his left foot. Sitting on the sidelines while his classmates danced was no fun for the little boy. Once his foot healed, Jonathan enrolled in another school, For Dancers Only, in Little Falls, just one town over from Totowa.

Every day after school he danced; weekends, he traveled to dance competitions.

"Almost every weekend," he remembers, "we'd go all over and I'd be in like 10 to 15 numbers. I had a solo in every category."

About the time that Jonathan started dance classes, Jane D'Annunzio left Jonathan's father. She ran her landscaping business during the week, and she got a weekend job as an after-hours nurse at a local doctor's office. That got her healthcare coverage for the family.

Because she owned her own business, she had the flexibility to chauffeur her youngest child to those dance classes and competitions. Sometimes she arrived straight from the jobsite, still dressed in her jeans and muddy boots.

"Because I was a single mom," she explains, "I could spend all my time devoted to him. I could spend whatever money I had on him. I didn't have to ask anybody, didn't have to get anybody's approval."

Her parents lived nearby, and they took care of her two older children, Joseph and Jaynie, when D'Annunzio and Jonathan were off at dance competitions. The two kids had their own activities: Joe was involved in sports and Jaynie had a large circle of friends. D'Annunzio says they didn't need her as much as Jonathan did.

Porretta at For Dancers Only, with Gina Marie Newarski and Erica Phifer Pelusio. Below: Porretta with teachers Eddie Phalen and Kelly Allen Angelo; Porretta with Evelyn Noland, who still runs the FDO studio today (Jane D'Annunzio photos)

Jonathan loved the time he spent in dance class, and he worked hard. Even after he moved to For Dancers Only, he remained the only boy among the girls. That felt natural to him.

One year, when he was eight or nine years old, Jonathan asked Santa to bring him a pair of pointe shoes for Christmas. That was all he wanted. D'Annunzio made sure that Santa brought her son his pointe shoes, but Santa also left Jonathan a note. "These pointe shoes are special, and probably you shouldn't bring them to dance class."

So Jonathan tied the satin ribbons at home, and pirouetted alone in his grandparents' large basement.

When he was 12 or 13, one of his teachers had him enroll in a pointe class; she wanted Jonathan to understand what girls had to endure to dance on their toes.

He loved that, too.

Porretta at age 12 with his mother, and at age 13
(images courtesy of Jane D'Annunzio)

Dance was Jonathan Porretta's refuge. It was also the place for him to shine. And he continued to reap accolades. In 1993, when he was 12 years old, the Dance Educators of America named him Junior Mr. Dance, a national honor. He won the same title the following year from a different competition organization. He had to dance a solo in the lyrical category, set to a song from the musical *Joseph and the Amazing Technicolor Dream Coat*. Three years later, the dance educators named him Teen Mr. Dance. The judges told his mother he had a future on Broadway. She preferred he pursue a ballet career, but for Jonathan, the possibility of his name on a Broadway marquee was tantalizing.

In his early teens, Jonathan saw his ballet classes as a means to an end: they'd help him polish his technique to prepare him for that Broadway career. He enrolled in a summer course at New Jersey Ballet School, but he kept his eyes on musical theater.

It wasn't that he didn't love ballet. Or ballet dancers. Jonathan cherished a book about the great Russian star Mikhail Baryshnikov. Baryshnikov was one of his idols. Along with the movie star Patrick Swayze.

———————

Jonathan Porretta's dance life was completely separate from the life he led at Totowa's Memorial School. In eighth grade, his final year there, Jonathan helped organize a talent show. And for the first time, he performed onstage in front of the very same classmates who had continued to shun him.

"Oh, the one time I was cool!" Porretta laughs. "I did a jazz dance, a solo. I went into a split; they thought it was amazing, and I was cool for about an hour."

The memory is much more bitter than sweet for his mother. "I remember him saying, 'Mom, how come all these years the kids hated me, and now when they saw me dance, they liked me?'"

Their opinions, good or bad, would cease to matter much after Jonathan finished eighth grade.

If you want to be a professional ballet dancer, you need to find the right school. And if you live in Totowa, New Jersey, or any place else in the United States for that matter, the right school is the School of American Ballet in Manhattan. It was founded in 1934 by Russian émigré choreographer George Balanchine to be the foundation of what would become Balanchine's professional company, New York City Ballet.

Every year, hundreds of aspiring dancers audition for a place at School of American Ballet. Few are chosen.

The way he tells it, Jonathan Porretta decided to audition for SAB on a lark. A girl from his school, For Dancers Only, asked him to go along with her, and he thought it would be fun.

"I didn't know about ballet tights, so I got girl tights—two pairs, with stirrups, over white socks and white shoes."

The kids lined up with hundreds of other hopefuls, numbers pinned to their chests. Former ballerina Suki Schorer, now on the School of American Ballet faculty, led the audition. Porretta remembers her stalking through the rows of aspiring dancers.

"One by one, she'd say, '*Tendu* front,' and she'd walk around and stretch you," says Porretta.

Fourteen-year-old Jonathan had studied dance for seven years, but he felt he was far less grounded in ballet technique than many of the other kids at the audition. Many of them had spent years learning ballet technique. Jonathan's training had been eclectic, with a focus on competitions, on jazz and Broadway styles.

But early on, Jonathan's Totowa Dance Center teacher, Miss Barbara, had pushed his body, forcing him into a routine of stretching his legs and feet. That discipline paid off for him at the audition. Ultimately, Jonathan was accepted to SAB on a four-year scholarship. His friend didn't make it.

"I was like, 'Thank you, Miss Barbara!'" he says.

School of American Ballet was a revelation for the young dancer who had spent so many years as the only boy at the barre.

"It was the first time in a class with all boys, and it was like, I'm not weird! There were lots of boys who were ballet dancers!"

Sexual orientation wasn't a big deal there, says Porretta. It was okay to be gay, or not to be gay. Ballet was what was important.

Academics became an afterthought. Like so many kids who train for professional ballet careers, Jonathan spent only half-days at his public high school. His weekday afternoons were devoted to dance.

Every day at lunchtime, D'Annunzio left work, picked up her son at Passaic Valley High School, and drove him into Manhattan to SAB. Then she turned around and went back to work. At the end of the day, she trekked back 20 miles from New Jersey to Manhattan to pick him up and bring him home.

Eighty miles. Every day. For two years.

Those long car rides provided many opportunities for conversations between mother and son.

Although Jonathan was thrilled to be part of the ballet world, he wasn't yet completely comfortable with himself. Even though he met other students who were gay, like many adolescents, Jonathan just wanted to fit in with the mainstream culture.

D'Annunzio remembers one conversation in particular. "He said, 'Mom, if there was a pill that could make me normal, I'd take it.'"

D'Annunzio was taken aback. "I remember whipping my head around and saying, 'Absolutely not!'"

Years later, D'Annunzio and Porretta laugh about this exchange. With the benefit of hindsight, and a successful ballet career, Porretta remarked to his mother, "Aren't you glad I never took that pill?"

If you are not a ballet-world insider, your mental images of the art form and the culture that surrounds it are probably gleaned from popular culture. Television shows depict backstabbing dancers who'll do anything to get ahead. Movies like *Black Swan* show us the mental toll that non-stop competition and a hothouse atmosphere can take.

Porretta says to forget everything you've seen. Competition at the School of American Ballet was stiff, but he and his friends weren't cutting themselves with mirror shards, or trying to sabotage each other. At SAB, he says, they thrived.

One of Porretta's classmates, Jordan Pacitti, admits, "It was cutthroat but it wasn't malicious." Pacitti says the students recognized that they were different from other teenagers.

"With ballet you're doing something special, different from the normal path of a teenager," Pacitti says. "You're competing with friends, but they're so close and you're so bonded!"

Both Pacitti and Porretta say SAB teachers expected students to be disciplined and to work hard. Most pupils anticipated ballet careers, but those with special talent were recognized. Porretta says Stanley Williams (a famous teacher whose students had included Rudolf Nureyev, Peter Martins, Edward Villella, and Mikhail Baryshnikov) created a top men's class. Participation was by invitation only.

According to Porretta, Williams chose young men he believed had the potential to be principal dancers someday. Porretta and Pacitti were part of that class.

Most SAB students lived in the school's Manhattan dorms; the few commuters like Porretta were accepted, but they weren't necessarily part of the school in-crowd. Pacitti remembers Porretta as a "good boy," but one day he was hanging out with a group of dorm kids, including Pacitti, at the back of a rehearsal studio.

"We were misbehaving," Pacitti laughs, "and we all got kicked out. And Jonathan was lumped in with us. He was mortified!"

Porretta didn't dare call his mother. Instead, he waited until the normal time she'd pick him up, then met her outside the school.

Peter Boal was a 31-year-old star with New York City Ballet at the time. He was asked to teach an intermediate men's class at SAB the year that Jonathan Porretta entered the school. Porretta was in that first class.

Boal remembers the teen as a class leader, with evident talent and technical abilities. Boal also remembers a teenager who thrived as a cut-up.

Porretta did everything his teachers asked of him. But sometimes, after he'd demonstrated his mastery of the day's combinations, Porretta would sneak off to the back of the studio. He'd run through Kitri's variations from *Don Quixote*, or whip off Odile's demanding *fouetté* turns from *Swan Lake*. Porretta loved to push himself; he enjoyed the technical demands, but what he really wanted was to make 'em laugh.

"It was funny," says Boal. "Even at that age, it was like, 'Oh, I think we need to rein him in!'"

"I'm always the jester, never the prince," Porretta still jokes.

In a world where tall, lean elegance defines ballet's romantic leading man, Porretta was short, dark, and compact. "My bio says I'm 5'9"," he says with a wink. Porretta's lack of stature and more traditional elegance pushed him to concentrate on technical mastery.

"I felt like I had to work twice as hard to be noticed," says Porretta. "I had to be perfect to make up for not being the tall, beautiful boy. Especially at SAB, where 'ballet is woman.' If you're a beautiful partner, you're in!"

Porretta learned to partner, but he really clamored for the athletic, challenging, jumping roles. He would work until his teachers noticed him.

Then-up-and-coming choreographer Christopher Wheeldon was tapped to make a piece for SAB stu-

dents. Wheeldon chose to set a *Scènes de Ballet* duet on Porretta and Pacitti. They performed its premiere as part of a full New York City Ballet program.

———

Like every SAB student, Porretta hoped for a job with New York City Ballet. NYCB dancers primarily have come up through SAB, so his dream wasn't so far-fetched. And given his participation in Stanley Williams' Special Men's class and the recognition he'd received from his teachers, Porretta had some confidence that he'd be hired. So when Ballet Master-in-Chief Peter Martins summoned him for a conversation one day, Porretta's heart skipped a beat. He was 18 years old, and he hoped he was about to be offered his dream job.

Instead, Martins told the young dancer he was simply too short to fit into the company's *corps de ballet*. Martins said, given the fact that he wouldn't be able to use Porretta in performances, he just couldn't hire him.

Porretta was devastated. But he took some consolation in Martins' assurances that he could get experience with another ballet company and possibly return to New York as a soloist in a few years. Representatives of dance companies regularly came to School of American Ballet looking for talented dancers, and Martins was sure one of them would happily hire Jonathan Porretta.

With that thought in the back of his mind, Porretta returned to the studio. He began to schedule auditions with some of the dance companies that visited New York City Ballet: Miami, Boston, East-Coast outfits.

The job at Pacific Northwest Ballet seemingly came out of nowhere.

One day, a teacher (Kay Mazzo) mentioned to Porretta that PNB Co-Artistic Director Francia Russell was coming to New York. Might he want to audition for the Seattle company?

The thought had never crossed his mind, but Porretta was game.

When the appointed day arrived, though, he was told Russell wasn't coming after all. With the pressure off, Porretta donned an oversized tee shirt and leg warmers and spent his class time goofing off. At one point, he vamped for his classmates, pretending to be then-NYCB star Darci Kistler, ultimately whipping off the 32 *fouetté* turns Odile performs in *Swan Lake*, ending with the *Dying Swan* pose.

Before he'd started, Porretta had noticed a well-dressed gentleman sitting in the front of the studio. He hadn't paid him much attention and didn't think to try to subdue his high energy. But when Porretta had finished his solo, a friend pulled him aside and asked if he knew who the gentleman was.

"Why should I?" Porretta responded.

That gentleman turned out to be Francia Russell's husband, and PNB's co-artistic director, Kent Stowell.

With five minutes left in the class, Porretta hastily ripped off the leg warmers and tee shirt and came out to show Stowell what he could do.

After class, Stowell met Porretta in the hallway and offered the teenager a contract.

Seventeen years later, Stowell remembers that Porretta had enchanted him.

"I do remember he was acting a little bit silly," says Stowell. "But it was endearing. The great thing about Jonathan is his exuberance. He loves to dance."

Porretta's height was absolutely not a concern, even though PNB had a reputation as a "tall" ballet company.

Porretta in the first *pas de trois* of George Balanchine's *Agon* with Kylee Kitchens and Elizabeth Murphy, and in Marco Goecke's *Mopey*, both at PNB (Angela Sterling photos)

"We didn't want a ballet company that was cookie cutter," Stowell maintains. "We'd prefer to have a talented dancer than the right size. And that fit Jonathan perfectly."

So, Porretta, who had never really left Totowa, New Jersey, except for dance competitions, packed up a few belongings and flew across the country to dance in Seattle. It was the farthest he'd ever been from his mother.

Seattle was a revelation. "I didn't know what to expect; I knew nothing about Seattle except episodes of *Frasier* I watched with my grandma!" Porretta jokes.

Porretta rented a tiny studio apartment, sight unseen, for $500 a month, more than a week's salary. His aunt came to town and helped him furnish the new place with castoffs from the building's basement. His television set was perched on a large cardboard box, covered with a scrap of cloth.

It was fabulous: Porretta had a job, a salary, and he was finally launched into the world of professional dance.

At Pacific Northwest Ballet, and many other professional companies around the country, first-year dancers are hired on as apprentices. They usually dance with the *corps de ballet* in ensemble roles; their future with the company is not guaranteed.

Porretta had arrived late for that 1999–2000 season; he'd been cast as a principal extra, a dancer, in the film *Center Stage*. He had to honor his commitment before he could move west. Most of the early-season dances had been cast by the time he got to PNB; Porretta didn't get a chance to be onstage until halfway through the season.

He knew that Stowell and Russell were watching him, watching his progress. He was nervous, but so thrilled to be dancing for an audience that he threw himself into the work. Just as he had done at School of American Ballet, Porretta spent hours at the barre, studying his movements in the mirror.

By January, Porretta had been cast in several featured roles. And he loved the Seattle company.

"I loved SAB," he says, "but I never felt like I quite fit in there." Porretta says he was loud and flamboyant in a place that was looking for restrained elegance.

"Coming to PNB, I felt very, very lucky, because I felt I fit right in. Kent and Francia made me feel that. Kent liked my jazzy side, how loud I was."

By the end of that first season, PNB offered him a *corps* contract.

"I remember on contract day, they handed it to me, I opened it, signed it, and handed it right back," Porretta laughs. "We have a month to decide. I didn't need to decide; I just signed."

This Seattle-based company, thousands of miles from New Jersey, fit him like a glove, in a way that New York never would.

"I was embraced for being me!" he says.

SAB classmate Jordan Pacitti joined PNB the same year as Porretta. And Porretta quickly befriended a young dancer from Pennsylvania, Carrie Imler, whom a New York friend had told him to meet. Those two PNB dancers became the nucleus of Porretta's new "family," a group that danced together, celebrated holidays together, and provided the emotional support Porretta had heretofore only gotten from his mother.

Porretta in Twyla Tharp's *In the Upper Room* and in David Parsons'
Caught (strobe light; collage), both at PNB (Angela Sterling photos)

Porretta abandoned any notion of returning to New York City Ballet. In Seattle, he danced a wide range of roles, from the title role in Balanchine's *Prodigal Son*, to a featured dancer in William Forsythe's *In the middle, somewhat elevated*. He loved the repertoire. And he loved everything about the place.

Francia Russell calls Porretta an ideal company member. He was diligent, disciplined, and most of all, open to criticism, suggestions, and corrections. "He trusted us and we trusted him. If there's real trust, a dancer can take chances," she says.

They gave Porretta more roles, featured roles. And they noticed he was a natural onstage, an audience favorite.

And despite his worries about how height might impact his partnering, Porretta found several steady partners: Imler, Noelani Pantastico, Kaori Nakamura. He has danced his share of princely roles, but that isn't where Porretta really shines. His true passion is the "hard roles, the harder the better!" He loves Balanchine's *Prodigal Son*, and his featured solo in Glen Tetley's *The Rite of Spring*. Porretta also adores the character roles: Puck in Balanchine's *A Midsummer Night's Dream*, Gamache in Alexei Ratmansky's *Don Quixote*, and the evil witch Carabosse in Ronald Hynd's *The Sleeping Beauty*.

He danced many of those roles the year before Russell and Stowell retired in 2005. Partly based on Porretta's performances that season, they promoted him to principal dancer.

Stowell says, simply, that Porretta deserved that promotion. "Because he's short...oftentimes those dancers get short shrift. He earned that position."

Porretta in Jean-Christophe Maillot's *Roméo et Juliette* with Batkhurel Bold at PNB (Angela Sterling photo)

The incoming Pacific Northwest Ballet artistic director, Peter Boal—Porretta's teacher at SAB—agrees with Stowell and Russell that the promotion was well deserved.

"One of the things I love about Jonathan," says Boal, "is that he throws himself into a role. He does his homework; he thinks about it."

More than commitment, Boal believes Porretta has something special that sets him apart from most dancers. It's a type of charisma you can't teach.

"He's riveting. You can't not watch him onstage," Boal explains. "When he walks out, somebody else could be front and center. But you're probably sneaking a peek at Jonathan from time to time."

Just take in a PNB performance of Alexei Ratmansky's *Don Quixote*. Porretta is not the handsome leading man; instead, he plays Gamache, the rich fop who vies for heroine Kitri's hand in marriage. While Kitri and her suitor, Basilio, court at one side of the big stage, Porretta's Gamache cavorts on a second-story balcony. Boal is correct: you can't stop watching him as he waggles a kerchief, hamming it up on the other side of the stage.

Hamming it up, yes—but Porretta's performance conveys more than camp. Gamache wants to wed Kitri, who spurns him. He is a devastated and angry man, as well as a silly fop, and a little part of every audience member feels the pain that Porretta conveys underneath all his histrionics.

When he's onstage, Jonathan Porretta finds his reward for all the years of hard practice, of painful rejection. As soon as he steps into the footlights, he tosses away the discipline of daily class, the hours of rehearsing each *tendu*, *battement*, and *jeté*. He can rely on his technique because he's worked so hard to

refine it. He no longer has to think; he just allows himself to move.

"It's better than sex. Better than anything," Porretta enthuses. "You can feel when the audience is in your corner. You can feel an energy going through you."

Boal believes Porretta lives most fully when he's on-stage. That's true for only a handful of people, in Boal's experience. "Nureyev was one. Wendy Whelan is another. They just lived more completely when they stepped onstage, and it's a really amazing thing to watch."

Which made 2015 a particularly agonizing year for Jonathan Porretta. In March, midway through PNB's production of an all-Forsythe program, an injury forced Porretta to stop dancing.

In 2013, he had developed bone chips in his foot. Although he underwent surgery that year, Porretta came back too quickly. His foot never fully recovered. This time, the pain was so intense that Porretta sidelined himself and sought medical help.

The bone chip had wedged its way between his joints, causing bone cysts in addition to major arthritis. The surgeon needed to remove the cysts, then take healthy bone from Porretta's heel to repair the damage. Porretta would need months of slow rehabilitation. The time out of the spotlight forced him to consider the inevitable for every dancer: retirement.

"I can't even talk about it. I can't," he sighs. "When you start this career the horizon is so far away, you never see the end. But when you get to a certain age—I'm 34 now—I can see it, and it's heartbreaking!"

Porretta hopes to dance until he's 40, but he's seen many good friends step down before they reach that age. He gives a little speech at every PNB retirement party. It's not a task he relishes; it's even harder to imagine somebody giving that same speech when he retires.

This time, Porretta has managed, through patience and perseverance, to stave off that unwelcome day. He obediently followed his doctor's orders, stayed off his foot, and only slowly returned to the PNB studios.

He's starting to think about his next career, after dancing. Maybe he'll teach, or coach dancers. Or open a cocktail lounge.

For now, though, Jonathan Porretta will cherish each performance. He has absolutely no regrets about the years of work, the childhood isolation, the mental and physical pain he has suffered.

"I had not one doubt from the first ballet class that this is what I wanted to do." He pauses to think.

"When I'm dancing, when I'm onstage, I'm just enjoying the moment. Onstage, I'm free." ✦

Porretta in Jerome Robbins' *Fancy Free* at PNB, with Glenn Kawasaki (Angela Sterling photo)

Roles, Guest Appearances & Choreography

Porretta in Ronald Hynd's *The Sleeping Beauty,* with Ezra Thomson and
Andrew Bartee in the background, at PNB (Lindsay Thomas photo)

38

ROLES AT SAB

Scènes de Ballet
Christopher Wheeldon

A Million Kisses to My Skin; Dances at a Gathering; A Midsummer Night's Dream with Carrie Imler and PNB company members; *Afternoon Ball* with Chalnessa Eames; all at PNB (Angela Sterling photos)

LEADING ROLES AT PNB

A Garden
Mark Morris

A Midsummer Night's Dream (Oberon, Puck)
George Balanchine

A Million Kisses to My Skin
David Dawson

Afternoon Ball
Twyla Tharp

Agon
George Balanchine

Amazed in Burning Dreams
Kirk Peterson

Ancient Airs and Dances
Richard Tanner

Artifact II
William Forsythe

Brief Fling
Twyla Tharp

Carmina Burana
Kent Stowell

Caught
David Parsons

Cinderella (Prince, Jester)
Kent Stowell

Circus Polka
Jerome Robbins

Concerto DSCH
Alexei Ratmansky

Coppélia (Franz)
George Balanchine

Cylindrical Shadows
Annabelle Lopez Ochoa

Dances at a Gathering
Jerome Robbins

Divertimento from "Le Baiser de la Fée"
George Balanchine

Don Quixote (Sancho Panza, Gamache)
Alexei Ratmansky

Emergence
Crystal Pite

Fancy Free
Jerome Robbins

Fearful Symmetries
Peter Martins

Forgotten Land
Jiří Kylián

Giselle (Peasant *pas de deux*)
Jean Coralli, Jules Perrot, Marius Petipa, and Peter Boal

Hail to the Conquering Hero
Kent Stowell

In the middle, somewhat elevated
William Forsythe

In the Upper Room
Twyla Tharp

Kammermusik No. 3
Mark Morris

Lambarena
Val Caniparoli

Memory Glow
Alejandro Cerrudo

Mercury
Lynne Taylor-Corbett

Mopey
Marco Goecke

New Suite
William Forsythe

Nine Sinatra Songs
Twyla Tharp

Nutcracker (Prince)
Kent Stowell

One Flat Thing, reproduced
William Forsythe

Paquita
Marius Petipa

Petite Mort
Jiří Kylián

Polyphonia
Christopher Wheeldon

Prodigal Son
George Balanchine

Red Angels
Ulysses Dove

Roméo et Juliette
Jean-Christophe Maillot

Rubies
George Balanchine

Sechs Tänze
Jiří Kylián

Serious Pleasures
Ulysses Dove

Silver Lining
Kent Stowell

The Four Temperaments (Melancholic)
George Balanchine

The Rite of Spring
Glen Tetley

The Sleeping Beauty
(Carabosse, Gold and Silver *pas de trois*,
Bluebird *pas de deux*)
Ronald Hynd

The Tragedy of Romeo and Juliet (Mercutio)
Kent Stowell

The Vertiginous Thrill of Exactitude
William Forsythe

Torque
Val Caniparoli

Voluntaries
Glen Tetley

Waterbaby Bagatelles
Twyla Tharp

Souvenirs
Todd Bolender

Square Dance
George Balanchine

State of Darkness
Molissa Fenley

Swan Lake (Jester)
Kent Stowell

Symphony in C
George Balanchine

Symphony in Three Movements
George Balanchine

TAKE FIVE…More or Less
Susan Stroman

The Ballad of You and Me
Lynne Taylor-Corbett

The Bridge
Val Caniparoli

The Concert
Jerome Robbins

One Flat Thing, reproduced with Jodie Thomas; *Sechs Tänze* with
Kylee Kitchens; *Roméo et Juliette*; *Rubies* with Leta Biasucci;
all at PNB (Angela Sterling photos)

ORIGINATED LEADING ROLES (PNB)

[soundaroundance]
Kevin O'Day

Almost Tango
Nicolo Fonte

arms that work
Andrew Bartee

Dual Lish
Kent Stowell

Opus 111
Twyla Tharp

Place a Chill
Marco Goecke

Quick Time
Christopher Stowell

Sum Stravinsky
Kiyon Gaines

Suspension of Disbelief
Victor Quijada

Time and other Matter
Dominique Dumais

Waiting at the Station
Twyla Tharp

Zaïs
Christopher Stowell

Suspension of Disbelief and *Opus 111* with Kiyon Gaines, both at PNB (Angela Sterling photos); *3Seasons* and *X stasis* with Lucien Postlewaite, both at Whim W'Him (Bamberg Fine Art photos)

SELECTED GUEST APPEARANCES

Dances Patrelle

Yorkville Nutcracker
(originated Snow Boy & Chinese)
Francis Patrelle

Ngoni (premiered The Narrator)
Francis Patrelle

Tango Plague (originated The Innocent)
Francis Patrelle

San Francisco Opera

Death in Venice
Michael Smuin, choreographer

Central Pennsylvania Youth Ballet

Stars and Stripes
George Balanchine

Oregon Ballet Theatre

Rubies
George Balanchine

Swan Lake (Prince Siegfried)
Christopher Stowell

Whim W'Him

3Seasons
Olivier Wevers

X stasis
Olivier Wevers
(*X stasis* premiered at PNB Choreographers'
Showcase and was also performed at
Against the Grain/Men in Dance Festival
and for Whim W'Him's inaugural performance.
Porretta danced in all three runs.)

CHOREOGRAPHY BY PORRETTA

The Four Elements
ca. 1996
for School of American Ballet

Duel
2004
for PNB's Choreographers' Showcase
leads: Carrie Imler and Melanie Skinner

Flawless
2005
for PNB's Choreographers' Showcase

Jubilant
2006
for PNB's Choreographers' Showcase

Lachrymosa
2008
for PNB's Choreographers' Showcase
leads: Chalnessa Eames and Seth Orza

Courte et Douce
2009
for PNB's Choreographers' Showcase

Spring Waltz
2010
for PNB's Choreographers' Showcase

Beila
2013
for PNB's Next Step

Jordan Pacitti with Josh Spell, Kara Zimmerman, Stacey Lowenberg, Rebecca Johnston, and Laura Tisserand in *Flawless*; Chalnessa Eames and Seth Orza in *Lachrymosa*; Kaori Nakamura and Lucien Postlewaite in *Jubilant*; Stacey Lowenberg, Kaori Nakamura, Lucien Postlewaite, and PNB company members in *Jubilant* (Rex Tranter photos)

The Highlights: 10 Key Roles

A Million Kisses to My Skin solo and *pas de deux* with Carrie Imler,
both at PNB (Angela Sterling photos)

David Dawson's

A Million Kisses to My Skin

Performed 9 times at PNB, 2012 & 2014
Performed 3 times on tour with PNB, 2014
Jacob's Pillow

Love. Love. The title says it all. It seriously does. It feels like a million kisses to your skin when you're done. It's a total rush. If I could have ever dreamed of a ballet, this would have been it. You know you're going to be wasted and exhausted at the end, but that's part of the whole adrenaline rush. I love it for how hard it is. I love it for the stamina and the athleticism.

The beauty of Dawson's choreography is amazing. He has exaggerated all the classical lines to be more free and it feels good. The flexed-flexed wrist and the giant-claw hand and everything being hyper-extended—it's like an overall body stretch.

I knew what it was going to be like before we learned it, because we had a video in the production office. When I saw my name on the cast list I was ecstatic. I loved the #3 Boy on the video and I got to do that part.

Tim Coachman was a dream stager. He was just amazing. He knew everything. He knew what to say to get the choreography across. He was loving and caring and nurturing but pushed you past what was comfortable. He made us feel safe enough to get out of our comfort zone—to get those extreme, contorted positions.

(I'm actually wearing his cologne right now. It's Aventus by Creed. I said I was going to get it, and [fellow PNB dancer] Sara Orza said, "You can't get that. That's Tim's scent!" We were obsessed with how good he smelled!)

The actual hardest part of *Kisses* for me is standing still during the second movement, facing the back scrim. I'm there for five to six minutes, not moving, panting, breathing heavily, feet cramping—just listening to the music and waiting for my time to turn around and start my *pas de deux*.

And my favorite part to dance? The third movement is awesome, but my opening—when I first walk out and look at Carrie and we both hit fifth-position *sous-sus*… It's a side-by-side duet. Everyone clears the stage and it's just us. After all this craziness, everything stops—and we hold in *sous-sus* for like five counts—and then we go into this cool duet that I love. It's fast. It's gooey. It's love.

—Jonathan Porretta

Prodigal Son with PNB company members (Angela Sterling photo);
the *Prodigal Son* jump for Men in Kilts 2014 (Lindsay Thomas photo);
posing à la *Prodigal Son* with Patricia Barker at a PNB gala in 2015 (photographer unknown)

George Balanchine's

Prodigal Son

Performed 7 times at PNB, 2004 & 2007
Performed 1 time on tour with PNB, 2016 New York

Edward Villella said it best: *Prodigal Son* is the male version of *Swan Lake*. It's a dream role. I used to go see Peter Boal perform it; I went to every show of his. I think I asked for his shoes. (I was like 14 or 15 at the time.) But I never got them. I was excited to perform it in New York [at City Center] in February 2016. That was a dream come true. I never thought I'd get to.

Prodigal Son has everything: the choreography, the music, the character, the acting: it really is a dream role. I love the *pas de deux*. It's incredible. It's amazing: Balanchine choreographed this in 1929 and it's still, now, so current and sexy and hard and challenging.

I love-love-*love* the ending, where there's no dancing any longer. You've been stripped of everything and it's just portraying this character.

The first time I did this ballet, I got to do it First Cast with Patricia Barker. I was a soloist still. That was incredibly scary and amazing at the same time. She was the prima ballerina of the company and one of my idols. She taught me a lot about partnering: holding hands a certain way, gripping things a certain way. Still, to this day, I use what she taught me.

There's a photo of me doing the *Prodigal Son* jump, but I don't like how my right knee is turned in. If you look at my Men

in Kilts picture, that's how it should look. I did that for the Ronald McDonald House fundraiser. Lindsay Thomas [the photographer] and I were trying to come up with masculine poses that look good in a skirt, and I said, "Let's do *Prodigal Son*, because we know it would look good in a kilt." We tried every year, trying to get the jump just right, and then—in our fourth year, in 2014—we nailed it.

Dick Tanner staged *Prodigal Son* for us the first time I did it. He was incredibly thorough; he knows the technical mechanics of the whole piece. I still do a lot of what he taught me from the first time. But since then, Peter has been staging it for us at PNB, and he has some different insights, especially on character development. He really goes into the emotional detail. Like in the end: Do you hear the water before you drink the water? Or do you smell the water? We spent a whole five minutes just working on cupping our hands and drinking water out of them. I love stuff like that. The magic is in the details.

—Jonathan Porretta

Square Dance solo and the finale with Jordan Pacitti, James Moore, Kiyon Gaines, and Barry Kerollis, both at PNB (Angela Sterling photos)

George Balanchine's

Square Dance

Performed 8 times at PNB, 2007, 2008, 2010 & 2016
Performed 1 time on tour with PNB, 2007 Vail

For me, it's all about the solo! My rep is mostly fast-paced and jumping—all about speed—so performing the *Square Dance* male solo is a complete opposite of what I have ever gotten to do on stage. I love it. It's one of the most beautiful solos a male dancer can get to do. There's nothing like it. It's very internal. It's very strong. But it's very gentle. And I've never gotten to slow down and show a softer side. I love the fast athletic stuff, but to get to show a different side of me is very fulfilling. It's like dancing a more princely role.

That solo lasts the perfect amount of time: four and a half minutes. I used to go and see Peter [Boal] do it at City Ballet all the time. I loved his elegance and grace. It was just beautiful to see a man being so graceful and beautiful but still so masculine and powerful. It was amazing. I've watched him so much

over 20 years—I've copied and stolen so much, honestly, that I don't know what's his or mine anymore.

The rest of *Square Dance* is pure fun for me. The whole beginning showcases *petit allégro*. I love all that fast footwork. *Petit allégro* is my favorite part of class. Nancy Bielski has the best *petit allégro* combos. Her combos just go on and on, and on and on and on. She's one of my favorite teachers ever. The first time I took her class was at an ABT summer course, when I was about 16 years old; I had her for two weeks and fell madly in love with her. So when I found out she taught at Steps, I would take any class with her that I could get. And it's helped me in my entire career, not just in *Square Dance*. Thanks, Nancy!

—Jonathan Porretta

In the middle, somewhat elevated with PNB company members and the *pas de deux* with Carrie Imler, both at PNB (Angela Sterling photos)

William Forsythe's

In the middle, somewhat elevated

Performed 11 times at PNB, 2000, 2006 & 2015
Performed 1 time on tour with PNB, 2007 Vail

It came to PNB my second year in the company, 2000–2001. I was 19, and I was Third Cast for Boy #3. (Again: Boy #3.) I never had seen a ballet like this ever. I was blown away that I got the opportunity to learn it. Third Cast never went on, but when the piece came back for PNB's season-ending *Encore* rep, due to some injuries I got to perform it with the company. I was only 20.

I call it the "original cool ballet." I had never seen an extreme version of classical ballet, ever. And I have never fallen in love with music quicker than I have with Thom Willems' score for that piece. I was so obsessed with this ballet that I got a recording on a cassette (because that's what we had back then!) and I listened to it every morning. I'd wake up and make coffee and I would listen to it, and that's how I'd get ready every morning, listening to *In the middle*. The only other person I know that is as obsessed with it as me is [PNB's ballet master] Otto Neubert; he has it as his ring tone.

Boy #3 gets to do the first solo. When I watched the video—before we learned the piece—I fell in love with that part. It has lots of *penchées* in it, and they can be really fun to do. There's cool jumps. And there are just really different things that I had never seen before. Like *A Million Kisses*, it's about making these big positions in quick time. It's extreme.

I love that first solo, but my favorite part is the *pas* with Carrie [Imler]. But anything I'm dancing with Carrie is probably my favorite part, to be honest. She's been my friend at the company since I first joined. She's one of my idols. We push each other. We're constantly trying to one-up each other, but in such a loving way. "Anything you can do, I can do better." That's Carrie and me. And that's what the whole Forsythe piece is, too.

Kathryn Bennetts staged it for PNB when we did it in 2015. And Forsythe came for two weeks, too. It was a dream come true, working with him. I couldn't wait! And then I got so sick that I couldn't come in for the first two days with Forsythe. I was home with a 102° fever. My entire career I had waited to work with him and then I had to miss the first two days! When I finally made it into the studio, he was everything that I could have dreamed him to be like. Incredibly kind and generous—and he just knew how to speak to you to pull different things out of you. He's a genius. He made me completely change my approach to the role. He stripped it down of anything extra the first few days, and little by little he would add flavors to it. By the time we got onstage, he told us to just go out there and kill it—to just go out there and have fun. And we did!

—Jonathan Porretta

Kent Stowell setting *Dual Lish* on Porretta and Noelani Pantastico at PNB (Angela Sterling photo);
Porretta and Pantastico in *Dual Lish* (Rex Tranter photo)

Kent Stowell's

Dual Lish

Performed 7 times at PNB, 2004 & 2005
Performed 2 times at the Guggenheim (NY) with PNB, 2005

Dual Lish started out as an enigma. I was called to a rehearsal with Kent Stowell [PNB co-artistic director] and Patricia Barker. Patty and I didn't know what was going on. She joked, "Are you learning my part?" I thought that would be the greatest thing! I'd love to learn her part!

We weren't going to dance together, I was sure, because of the height difference; if Kent was going to choreograph a *pas de deux* for Patty, it wouldn't be with me. But that partnership only lasted for one rehearsal. We basically just played around in the studio for Kent and did choreography with him. It turns out he was just workshopping with us.

About a month later, rehearsal for *Dual Lish* started, and it was Noe [Pantastico] and me. It was the last ballet Kent was going to choreograph for PNB; we knew that at the time and we felt very privileged.

It's more of a duet than a *pas de deux*. It's like a little competition between the two of us. The two pianos onstage are dueling at the same time: they're dueling and we're dueling. There was one point where Noe and I slapped our thighs (*ba da ba dum*), and one time I slapped Dianne [Chilgren, one of the pianists] instead, on the last beat, on purpose, as a joke, and she of course loved it because she's a ham herself. And Kent loved it, so we kept that in. I used to run over and play on Dianne's piano, too—*ding! ding! ding! ding!* But Kent didn't keep that in.

Noe and I used to joke-fight over who was going to get the rights to this ballet. She'd say, "Well, I'm the girl, so I get it." And I'd say, "I started working on it first, so I get it." We would say, "Who was it more choreographed for, you or me?" Which is silly. It was tailored to both of us, to our personalities.

I adore this ballet. I would love to dance this again. It was a fun, jazzy piece. It was very Kent. It was Kent at his best, at his most fun. It's just a happy piece. It's like you're in a bar, having a good time.

—Jonathan Porretta

A Midsummer Night's Dream: As Oberon, with Carrie Imler and PNB company members; as Puck with Bottom (unidentified); and as Puck; all at PNB (Angela Sterling photos)

George Balanchine's

A Midsummer Night's Dream

Performed 18 times at PNB, 2004, 2007, 2008 & 2011
Performed 1 time on tour with PNB, 2002 Hollywood Bowl

The first time I saw *Midsummer*, I immediately fell in love with [NYCB soloist] Tom Gold and the character of Puck. It was the first ballet other than *Nutcracker* that I saw at City Ballet. I remember dancing as Puck in the hallway and elevator on the way to get the car. I remember ranting and raving about it—how he flew at the end. The way that Tom Gold did it was so beautiful: he went up in a harness, and touched his head back to his foot. It was just amazing; it was like he just folded in half. From then on, he was the dancer I wanted to be when I grew up. Baryshnikov had been my idol since I was a little kid, but Tom I saw live, right in front of my eyes. It was like seeing a real, live superhero.

Cut to years later: The first time I was cast in *Midsummer* at PNB, I was on Cloud 9. I was Puck. And I got to perform it for the first time at the Hollywood Bowl, when we did some excerpts for *Shakespeare at the Bowl*. It was outdoors. It was incredible. And I got to meet Michael York; he narrated it. I have a picture of me and Louise Nadeau (who danced Titania), and who's lurking in the background? Michael York! He totally photo-bombed my picture!

(See photo on page 85.) He was very cool. And even better? Julie Andrews was there, at the show. I got to meet her; she came backstage and was…Julie Andrews! Incredibly gracious, beautiful, and kind.

The next time *Midsummer* came back, I was cast for both Puck and Oberon. I always joke that I don't get to be the prince, but I do get to be the king. And it's good to be the king. Oberon is an ultimate favorite role of mine. I've said that I love *petit allégro*, and this is the ultimate *petit allégro* part. The *scherzo* is the main dancing part for Oberon, and it's a series of four short solos, all *petit allégro*—lots of beats and jumping and quick timing. I love it, I love it, I love it! I love the whole thing. I guess the beat *sissonnes* are my favorite, but I love the whole thing.

Oberon or Puck? I can't pick a favorite. There's no picking.

—Jonathan Porretta

Rehearsing *State of Darkness* with Molissa Fenley at PNB;
with Emil de Cou and Peter Boal at dress rehearsal (Angela Sterling photos)

Molissa Fenley's

State of Darkness

Performed 6 times at PNB, 2007 & 2014
Performed 2 times with Molissa Fenley and Company, 2014
Performed 1 time on tour with PNB, 2014 Jacob's Pillow

Mar-a-thon! I love hard, stamina pieces; they're my favorite. And this one is 34 minutes long. I love the physical endurance. I want to be exhausted and dripping with sweat at the end; I feel accomplished then. It's an adrenaline high, just knowing what you have to accomplish and how you're going to get there.

State of Darkness taught me a lot about pacing myself and about breathing. When I was younger, I felt like I gave 150 million percent to every step. Now, it's about artistry and shading. If you take 50 percent here and 100 percent there, then that 100 percent reads even bigger. That's what I learned doing *State of Darkness*. You couldn't finish it otherwise.

The hardest thing is the mental preparation. To wrap your brain around the idea that you're going to be onstage for 34 minutes was really scary at first. But now it kind of goes in the blink of an eye. *State of Darkness* now feels like a second layer of skin on me. The first time I performed it, though, I was constantly thinking of what was coming next. Thirty-four minutes! You're out there alone. You're screwed if you forget anything. There's no one to rescue you.

Actually, the first time we did it, Rachel [Foster], James [Moore], and I stood in the first wing for each other for the whole 34 minutes. So if you forgot a step or got lost in the choreography, they were there in the wing to help you through it. It was our way of comforting each other. Nobody else knew how we felt; during *State of Darkness* we were very alone. I was only the third person to ever perform it. Molissa did it in 1988, and Peter [Boal] did it in 1999. James and Rachel were fourth and fifth. It's like being in a very exclusive club. It was a really amazing bonding experience for the three of us. We used to talk about the choreography together. Molissa helped; she even took us out. We went to the sculpture park and talked about the pieces we saw—how they can all be reflected with movements. She was trying to make everything sculptural in *State of Darkness*.

Getting to go to New York and perform it for Molissa's company was an honor.

I'd love to do this for my retirement performance.

Did I mention it's 34 minutes?

—Jonathan Porretta

Rubies at PNB (Angela Sterling photo);
with Edward Villella at New Jersey Ballet School (photo courtesy of Jane D'Annunzio);
with Edward Villella at dress rehearsal at PNB (Angela Sterling photo)

George Balanchine's

Rubies

Performed 6 times at OBT, 2003
Performed 10 times at PNB, 2006, 2009, 2011 & 2014
Performed 1 time on tour with PNB, 2007 Vail

The first time I found out I was doing *Rubies*, I was a soloist. It was during an intermission of *Nutcracker* at the Paramount Theatre, when we were in transition here [renovating McCaw Hall]. Christopher Stowell, one of Kent and Francia's sons, came up to me backstage in the wings and asked if I'd be interested in coming to guest for him at Oregon Ballet Theatre. My initial reaction was excitement, but the first thing I said to him was, "But is it OK with your parents?"

The first time I saw *Rubies*, I was 12 or 11—it was before I was even at SAB. I went to see City Ballet, and I was all excited. I may have fallen asleep during *Emeralds*—nothing against *Emeralds*!—but when *Rubies* started, I was on the edge of my seat the entire time. I didn't think ballet actually looked like that. I fell in love with it. I thought *Diamonds* was amazing, too, but my favorite of the whole night was *Rubies*.

Flash forward to learning it at OBT, from Colleen Neary. She was the first stager I learned it with. She was amazing. I loved working with her. She's this tall, strikingly beautiful ballerina; she knew everything inside and out. It was one of the smoothest stagings ever.

It was just an exciting time for me in my career, getting to go back and forth between OBT and PNB, dancing this amazing role with Yuka Iino, who was a technically beautiful dancer and one of the sweetest and most humble. It was pretty sick; I felt so cool.

And since then, I've danced it many, many times, and it never gets old. Each time it's been with a

different partner: Yuka Iino was the first. And then, in no particular order, because I love them all: Kaori Nakamura, Jodie Thomas, Chalnessa Eames, Miranda Weese, Leta Biasucci. Six partners. Each one taught me something different about the role. It was always a pleasure and so much fun to dance.

When we did it at PNB in 2014, I got to work with Edward Villella. I had been looking forward to working with him since I was a kid. I feel like so many of my favorite roles are roles that he originated or that he starred in. I have a picture with him teaching my class at New Jersey Ballet, and I had him sign my *Prodigal Son* book back then. So I had him sign it again, this time at PNB. I was kind of like his stalker this time around, telling him this story and showing him the picture of us from when I was a kid. He was really nice to me, but he may have been afraid of me.

He hasn't changed since that first class that I took with him all those years ago. He puts out the same amount of energy that he always did. He was the same charming, exuberant, charismatic artist. The way he helped Leta [Biasucci] and me, working on the choreography—but always with a story from when it was choreographed on him. And what's amazing is what he can get across—how he helped us interpret his stories into the choreography. We got a real blueprint from the original instead of a carbon copy.

If you ever get to dance *Rubies*, just enjoy it. It's a treasure.

—Jonathan Porretta

Agon at PNB (Angela Sterling photos)

George Balanchine's

Agon

Performed 7 times at PNB, 2005, 2007 & 2013
Performed 4 times on tour with PNB, 2008 Santa Fe, 2013 New York & Victoria

When I first joined PNB, *Agon* was one of the first ballets that they were doing here. I was taught the male solo at SAB and dreamed of dancing it. I guess I was very ballsy: I went and asked Francia [Russell, PNB co-artistic director] if I could come to rehearsal. At 18. I wasn't really in a "cast;" I just went into the studio to learn it.

One day, there happened to be time left at the end of rehearsal, and Francia asked me if I wanted to rehearse the solo with her. And so I did. It was really amazing that she took the time to do that. It was everything to me.

I hadn't picked up the small changes that PNB did, and so I did the version that I had learned at SAB. Francia let me finish, and then we went through and just polished it and changed it to the version we were doing here: little changes, like one arm was down instead of up, things like that. I was blown away that I got to rehearse with her at 18, on a role that I wasn't even cast for.

A few years later, the ballet came back and I was Third Cast for the solo. I was still in the *corps*!

The whole ballet in general is just so fierce without trying to be anything except ballet. It's just straightforward—intricate, but not trying too hard. It's brilliant. The main *pas de deux* is one of the most amazing pieces of choreography; to this day, it is incredible. It was so ahead of its time. And it's sexy—and beautiful. To dance in a piece that is so brilliant feels just amazing.

I had seen City Ballet do it numerous times and dreamed about doing the Peter Boal part [the first *pas de trois*]. He was technically fierce; I wanted to dance it. I had no idea what was in store for me with the counts!

I prefer not to count—though I don't mind for a Balanchine ballet. (I have a clause in there for a Balanchine ballet!) They are so complex, and somehow the counts and the choreography work in unison. I don't feel like it's like that for all ballets, which is why I would prefer to listen to the music and dance to it, usually. But for the Stravinsky and Balanchine combo, it works just perfectly.

—Jonathan Porretta

The Rite of Spring at PNB (Angela Sterling photo);
note from Glen Tetley (Jonathan Porretta photo)

Glen Tetley's

The Rite of Spring

Performed 5 times at PNB, 2005

I remember this period of my life so vividly. We were told in class that certain dancers were going to have to come back from Christmas break a week early so that they could rehearse *The Rite of Spring*. I was a soloist—I was only 24—so I didn't think it involved me. And after that class, Francia pulled [Batkhurel] Bold and me aside. I was ecstatic. I had to change my plane ticket and come back early from Jersey.

They got the video shortly after that. (VHS!) When I looked at it, my head exploded. I couldn't believe I had been picked to do this ballet. I stayed in the production office for hours, watching that video. There are three main solos for the Chosen One—that was the character I got to do. The dancer on the video was spectacular. I was blown away by him—by the choreography, by his stamina, by the circular, animalistic movements: I couldn't wait to dance this!

The rehearsal process was really cool. And it was very difficult. We worked with this awesome lady named Bronwyn Curry. She had this way of saying, "Groovy, groovy, baby." We had to do everything groovy. She could undulate every part of her body. I thought everything I did was terrible. I tried every step the way I used to approach, well, everything—maybe a bit too energetically—and Bronwyn would ask me to calm things down. For example, for the *saut de chat*, I was splitting my legs too much. She wanted them to get to the split, but not with a *swack*; it had to be slower, like a *whoosh*. There was a lot of hanging in the air.

I loved being up in the air. It was so much fun. In the end, I was on a trapeze! I was supposed to be going up to heaven. I got hazard pay for that. Ha ha, extra pay for extra fun.

There is a part in one of the solos that Bronwyn would describe as a *cabriole*. "You just *cabriole*," she'd say, "and you fly and you gracefully [!] land on the floor, on your face." You do that pass two times in a row. [See photo on page 77.] Really it's about trick-

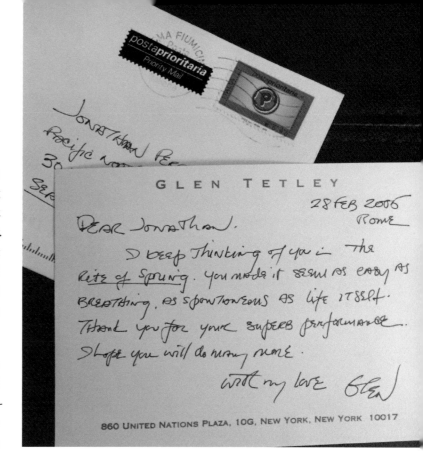

ing your brain out: it's about superman-ing yourself into the air and you just have to do it. I remember Ariana [Lallone] watching me land, always asking me if my hip was OK. I was young, so everything was fine at that time.

I didn't even know if I was going to get to perform this ballet because of how hard Bronwyn was on me during the staging. The first day that Glen Tetley arrived, we did a run-through for him. And the first thing he said after the run-through was a compliment to me in front of the entire company, and I was, like, in tears because I didn't think I had been doing well. Bronwyn had been pushing me to be the best I could be in this part. She had just been coaching me.

I could talk about this ballet forever. It was probably the most intense role I've ever done. I have never felt more like a rock star in my life than bowing for this ballet. It was the coolest ovation of my entire career. I wish this ballet would come back, but I don't know if I'd survive it!

About a month after the show, I went to check the dancers' mailbox at PNB and I found this note [above] from Glen Tetley. I almost passed out.

—Jonathan Porretta

Chronology

1981

Born in Wayne, NJ, at 9:20 a.m. on May 30

1984

Attended *The Nutcracker* at New York City Ballet; decided to become a dancer

1988

Parents divorced; began dance classes with Miss Barbara Bruno at Totowa Dance Center

1989

First pair of pointe shoes

1992

Began classes at For Dancers Only (in Little Falls, New Jersey) at 11, under the direction of Kelly Allen Angelo (teachers included Edward Phalen)

1993

First of two years of pointe class

1994

Named Junior Mr. Dance by Dance Educators of America at 13; enrolled in summer program at New Jersey Ballet School (teachers included Edward Villella); helped organize a talent show at Memorial School in Totowa, NJ

1995

Began attending classes at School of American Ballet (Boys 3 and Intermediate Men's) at age 14; half-days at Passaic Valley High School

1996

Continued at SAB; named Teen Mr. Dance by Dance Educators of America; choreographed first ballet (*The Four Elements* for SAB studio performance)

1997

Advanced classes at SAB; invited to Stanley Williams' Special Men's class at SAB; started high school correspondence coursework; attended American Ballet Theatre summer course (first of two summers there); took his first Nancy Bielski class; lived alone in San Francisco for one month, dancing in San Francisco Opera's *Death in Venice*

1998

Performed in the premiere of Christopher Wheeldon's *Scènes de Ballet*

1999

Cast by Christopher Wheeldon as a principal extra, a dancer, in the film *Center Stage;* joined Pacific Northwest Ballet at 18 as an apprentice

2000

Cast in soloist and principal roles in *Silver Linings* and *In the middle, somewhat elevated* at Pacific Northwest Ballet; toured with PNB to Hong Kong and Istanbul; promoted to *corps de ballet*

2002

Promoted to soloist at Pacific Northwest Ballet at 21; performed his first Puck at the Hollywood Bowl with PNB; toured to London with PNB

2003

Danced his first *Rubies* as a guest at Oregon Ballet Theatre

2004

Choreographed *Duel* for PNB's Choreographers' Showcase; Kent Stowell choreographed his last ballet for PNB on Porretta and Noelani Pantastico

2005

Promoted by Kent Stowell, Francia Russell, and Peter Boal to principal at Pacific Northwest Ballet at 24; performed at the Guggenheim *Works & Process*: *Dual Lish* with Jodie Thomas, *Hail the Conquering Hero*, and "Melancholic" from *Four Temperaments*; choreographed *Flawless* for PNB's Choreographers' Showcase; performed *Prodigal Son* for the first time (with Patricia Barker on opening night); performed Glen Tetley's *The Rite of Spring*

2006

Choreographed *Jubilant* for PNB's Choreographers' Showcase

2007

Danced his first *State of Darkness* (at PNB, working with Molissa Fenley)

2008

Worked with Twyla Tharp for the first time (*Opus 111* and *Afternoon Ball);* choreographed *Lachrymosa* for PNB's Choreographers' Showcase

2009

Choreographed *Courte et Douce* for PNB's Choreographers' Showcase; taught at Central Pennsylvania Youth Ballet summer session; underwent surgery to repair a medial meniscus tear

2010

Choreographed *Spring Waltz* for PNB's Choreographers' Showcase

2012

Toured to Spoleto Festival dei Due Mondi with PNB

2013

Choreographed *Beila* for PNB's Next Step; first foot surgery (left foot, fractured bone: removal of bone spurs and chips); began teaching at Evergreen City Ballet

2015

Coached by William Forsythe on *In the middle, somewhat elevated, New Suite,* and *The Vertiginous Thrill of Exactitude;* second foot surgery (same left foot, removed bone cysts that had developed from coming back too soon after the first surgery); seven-month recovery

2016

Returned to the stage in February as Mercutio in PNB's *Roméo et Juliette;* performed *Prodigal Son* and *The Vertiginous Thrill of Exactitude* on PNB's New York tour in February

Selected Bibliography

By the time a reviewer has covered the who-what-where-when of a ballet performance, there usually isn't much room left to describe the impact of individual dancers. Alas, sometimes the best a reviewer can do is slip in a short phrase for the standouts.

The many one-line mentions of Jonathan Porretta (not included in this selected bibliography) paint a vivid picture. When Porretta was only 15, the *Village Voice* mentioned his "pristine technique." *The New York Times* review of an SAB recital two years later says Porretta and two cohorts "nearly stole the show." He is "ultra-nimble and vivacious" in the London *Sunday Times* and "hyper-alert" in the *Financial Times*. His *Prodigal Son* moved Wendy Perron of *Dance* to tweet: "Jonathan Porretta just slayed me... From bounding joy to pathetic despair." Locally, we love him too: "This man soars like a superhero," says the *Seattle Times*. The *Seattle Weekly* puts Porretta in perspective: "He makes the stage seem small."

—Rosie Gaynor

ARTICLES

April 29, 1997
The Village Voice by Kate Mattingly
"Players in the Field"

July 1, 2002
criticaldance.com by Stuart Sweeney
"An Interview with Jonathan Porretta, Soloist, Pacific Northwest Ballet"

October 31, 2003
Seattle Post-Intelligencer by R.M. Campbell
"Poretta's [sic] Making His Presence Felt at Pacific Northwest Ballet"

January 2005
ballet-dance.com by Dean Speer & Francis Timlin
"Jonathan Porretta, Soloist, Pacific Northwest Ballet: Tri-State Native, All-State Soloist"

July 2005
Dance Magazine by Gigi Berardi
"On the Rise: Jonathan Porretta"

June 2009
Dance International (web post; reposted on SeattleScriptorium.com/content.html)
by Rosie Gaynor
"Jonathan Porretta: A Showman Finds the Artist Within"

December 2009/January 2010
Pointe by Rosie Gaynor
"The Standouts, 2009"

December 2013/January 2014
Pointe by Zachary Wittenburg
"And Now From the Men…"

October 2014
Dance Magazine by Jonathan Porretta
"Why I Dance"

December 2014
DanceSpirit by Amy Smith
"Dealing With Casting Disappointments"

Fall 2015
IEEE Engineering Management Review
by Rosie Gaynor
"Mining Management Ideas in Unexpected
Places: Ballet"

December 2015/January 2016
Pointe by Marcie Sillman
"Truly Exceptional: Our Top 12 Standout
Performances of 2015"

January 12, 2016
KUOW.org by Marcie Sillman
"The Tiny Dancer Who Became a Big Star
in Seattle"

Spring 2016
Wayne Magazine by Adriana Mariella
"One Dancer's Dream"

SIGNIFICANT MENTION

June 2, 2007
Seattle Post-Intelligencer by Alice Kaderlan
"Jonathan Porretta Soars in an Explosive Role"

June 6, 2007
Queen Anne News by Rosemary Jones
"Solo Performance, Jonathan Porretta a Knockout
Dancing Molissa Fenley's 'State of Darkness'"

March 26, 2007
The New York Times by Jennifer Dunning
"It's Not Your Mother-in-Law in a Tutu, but She
Dances"

January 2014
City Dog by Deanna Duff
"Dancers & Dogs"

February 26, 2016
The New York Times by Alastair Macaulay
"Basking in Balanchine's Space-Time Continuum"

LEAD IMAGE IN GENERAL REVIEW, ARTICLE, OR LISTING

June 7, 1999, *The New York Times*

Fall 2001, *Dance International*

June 3, 2002, *Seattle Post-Intelligencer*

March 15, 2003, *The Seattle Times*

October 15, 2004, *The Columbian*

September 23, 2006, *The Seattle Times*

July 31, 2007, *Vail Daily*

Fall 2007, *Dance International*

February 21 & 26, 2016, *The New York Times*

Encore

Porretta in rehearsal with William Forsythe at PNB; Kyle Davis and
Chelsea Adomaitis in the background (Angela Sterling photo)

80

Left (clockwise): Porretta with Jane D'Annunzio (mom); with Joey (brother) and Jaynie (sister); with Kathy Marmo (the family friend who helped pay for his first dance classes); with his aunt, Carol D'Annunzio; with mom and Joseph M. Porretta (dad); with sister and brother. **Above:** Porretta on his mother's back at around 8 months, with a family friend on Nibbles; with Jaynie, Steve Drehetz (stepdad), and Joey; with Jaynie. **Below:** Dressed as a unicorn; with unicorn tattoo; playing street hockey with Joey, one house down from their childhood home.

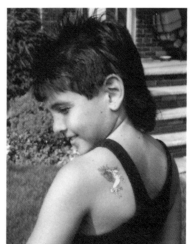

Above: Porretta with his dog, Angelo; with Royal (horse) and with Crystal (cat); with his family in Florida (Joey, Jaynie, and Jane). **At right:** Porretta with mom, Jane D'Annunzio, on various occasions through the years; arriving in Seattle the first time; outside PNB; with niece Cheyann during PNB's February 2016 New York tour (photos courtesy of Jane D'Annunzio)

Clockwise from top left: Porretta's first time surfing; dressed as the White Queen for Halloween; Paco Card: Porretta did a stock-photo shoot for Getty Images, and that image showed up on (among other things) this card that Jordan Pacitti received from Noelani Pantastico; recuperating from surgery with Angelo in 2015; with Kiyon Gaines; after Zumba class with Benjamin Griffiths, Kiyon Gaines, Melanie Skinner (teacher), and Josh Spell; with Chalnessa Eames during a break in rehearsal at PNB; Superman socks worn regularly in class; with Kaori Nakamura in class at PNB on Halloween. (All photographers unknown except socks by Toby Smith, rehearsal by Marcie Sillman.)

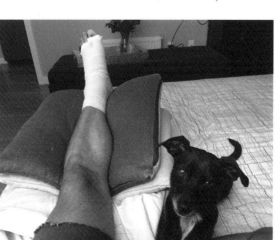

Above: Porretta with Alessandra Ferri during PNB's Spoleto tour; with Louise Nadeau and Michael York at the Hollywood Bowl. **Below:** Backstage fun at PNB; *Rocky Horror* Halloween with Josh Spell. **Right:** Porretta with longtime boyfriend Sean Stroupe; with Molissa Fenley after *State of Darkness* at Jacob's Pillow; with Violette Verdy at PNB; with Leta Biasucci after guesting for *Nutcracker*; with Tom Skerrit after *Don Quixote* at PNB; with Ariana Lallone at Teatro Zinzanni (photographers unknown)

Left: Porretta with Kiyon Gaines and Josh Spell; with Carrie Imler; with Kaori Nakamura; with Chalnessa Eames; with Jordan Pacitti; with Noelani Pantastico. **Above, clockwise:** Stretching with Lindsi Dec on the way home from Jacob's Pillow; *Coppélia* rehearsal, with Margaret Mullin, Lesley Rausch, and Leta Biasucci (Noelani Pantastico photo); backstage after *A Million Kisses to My Skin* (Lindsay Thomas photo); choreographer's bow at PNB's Next Step (Rex Tranter photo); backstage during a PNB gala, playing *Prodigal Son* with Jordan Pacitti; in Capri with (left to right) Sean Stroupe, Jordan Pacitti, [Porretta], Sarah Ricard Orza, Seth Orza, Jérôme Tisserand, Laura Tisserand, and Benjamin Griffiths.

Porretta in Jean-Christophe Maillot's *Roméo et Juliette*,
with Benjamin Griffiths, James Moore, and Seth Orza
at PNB (Angela Sterling photos)

Porretta with some of his partners
(clockwise from left):
Jodie Thomas in *Rubies*
Yuko Iino in *Swan Lake Act III* (OBT)
Kaori Nakamura in *Coppélia*
Chalnessa Eames in *Giselle*
Leta Biasucci in *Rubies*
Noelani Pantastico in *Square Dance*
Carrie Imler in *Opus 111*
(OBT photo by Blaine Truitt Covert;
all other photos at PNB by Angela Sterling)

Porretta's comic side (from bottom left to right): *Sechs Tänze* with James Moore; *Nine Sinatra Dances* with Carrie Imler; *The Sleeping Beauty:* 4 photos (Lindsay Thomas photos); *The Concert*: 1 photo with Miranda Weese (seated), 1 photo with Jordan Pacitti in the background, 2 photos solo; *Don Quixote* with members of the cast (all at PNB; Angela Sterling photos unless noted otherwise)

Photoshoot with Marc von Borstel for Whim W'Him
(left) and photoshoots with Lindsay Thomas for the
Ronald McDonald House fundraiser Men in Kilts (right)

About the Author

Marcie Sillman has been covering the Seattle arts scene for 30-plus years. Her work is heard in Seattle on the NPR-affiliate KUOW FM, and it has also appeared in the *Seattle Times*, *Crosscut*, and on the Seattle Channel.

Nationally, she reports for NPR and has written for *Pointe* and *Dance Teacher* magazines.

She was the recipient of a National Endowment for the Arts fellowship in dance journalism in 2009.

More of Sillman's writing can be found on her blog, *And Another Thing*, at marciesillman.com.

Acknowledgements

Jonathan Porretta

Jane D'Annunzio

Toby Smith

Laurie Griffith

Glenn Kawasaki

Aya Hamilton

Gail James

Alan Lande

Jordan Stead, Lindsay Thomas, Rex Tranter, Marc von Borstel

Lisa Gordanier, Sandra Kurtz, Anna Waller

Bond Huberman, Julie Paschkis, Patti Smithson

Pacific Northwest Ballet

Sandy Barrack, Marsha Bennion, Sheila Dietrich, Doug Fullington, Gary Tucker

KUOW and KUOW staff, especially Isolde Raftery and Jim Gates

Kent Stowell and Francia Russell

Jeff Barlow

The School of Visual Concepts

Kate Farwell, Tina Ryker, Amy Scott

Suzanne Carbonneau and the NEA Dance Journalism Institute at
Duke University/American Dance Festival

Special thanks to Dr. Nicholas Seibert for reconstructing Porretta's foot and to
Boyd Bender, Henry Lu, and Karin Townson for keeping his body in motion—
and to Larae Theige Hascall and the PNB Costume Shop for the extra love they
put into his costumes.

Porretta on his first day of rehearsal with William Forsythe after being home sick
with a 102° fever (2015), at PNB; Sarah Pasch, Elle Macy, and Lindsi Dec in the
background (Angela Sterling photos)

Jonathan Porretta and I spoke frequently in the fall of 2015. He was recuperating from the foot surgery he'd undergone that summer, and had nothing but time on his hands to answer my questions about his childhood and his career.

But Porretta's mind was set on the future, rather than the past. He wanted to be back on stage. And nobody could tell him exactly when that would happen.

For Porretta, the months out of the studio were clearly not only about physical therapy. They were a lesson in patience for this man who lives to dance.

"How're you doing?" I'd ask him.

"80 percent there," he'd answer. The next time I saw him, he'd tell me he was 90 percent healed.

The November rep came, and went. So did the 30-plus performances of *The Nutcracker*.

By December, Porretta was back in company class on a regular basis.

One day I peeked through the windows and noticed he was holding back during the jumping portion of the daily regimen.

I felt a bit like I was watching a race horse in the starting gate at the Kentucky Derby.

Porretta's mind was focused on performing in Jean-Christophe Maillot's *Roméo et Juliette* in early February, but his body craved dancing there and then.

On February 5, 2016, I was in Marion Oliver McCaw Hall for *Roméo et Juliette*'s opening night. The ballet is beloved in Seattle, so the audience was abuzz with anticipation.

I held my breath, waiting for Porretta. He was cast in the role of Mercutio; all tease and swagger, it was a perfect fit for him. It was no secret that his character would die tragically later on, but when Porretta twirled onstage for the first time, to the applause of the audience who'd missed him for so many months, I could sense his joy.

And I was delighted to see this man doing what he was born to do: dancing for us.

—Marcie Sillman

be loved for who you are

CPSIA information can be obtained at www.ICGtesting.com
Printed in the USA
BVIW12n0532220816
459749BV00001B/1